# Social Media for Scientists

## Engaging the Public

# Table of Contents

So next time you see a scientist, give them a big hug, say 'Thank you.' And then, before she can run away, quickly ask her to explain dark matter to you.

— Neil deGrasse Tyson

# Chapter 1. Introduction

Welcome to an invigorating Special Report tastefully brewed for the curious minds in the labs and beyond, titled "Social Media for Scientists: Engaging the Public"! In an era where digital interactions are the norm, the worlds of science and social media collide in an enlightening fusion, opening avenues for extraordinary public engagement. This crucial report walks you through how you, as scientists, can efficaciously engage with the public and elucidate your complex breakthroughs in an easily understandable and attractively digestible format. Whisk away those lab coats and let's dive into a riveting exploration of building narratives, crafting social media strategies, and learning to "tweet" your science to a world eagerly awaiting. Fun, engaging, and replete with insights, this report is as delightful as it is informative, so much so you will wish you had it sooner! Just delve in, and let the journey of engagement beyond the lab begin!

# Chapter 2. Demystifying Social Media for Scientists

In this vast ocean of digital communication, we find social media platforms becoming detonating beacons of catharsis, connection, and communication. For scientists, however, these platforms can appear as mystifying galaxies spinning out of their orbital control. But fret not, because we are all star explorers who fathom profound mysteries, aren't we? Demystification comes naturally to our kind. Endeavoring on this exploration, we shall anatomize various aspects of social media, understand what they are, and gain an insight into their tremendous potential if harnessed judiciously.

## 2.1. What is Social Media?

We stand at the cusp of a technological revolution, viewing the world through the prism called social media. Understanding what it is forms the very foundational brick in this wall of interaction. Simply put, social media, that grand tapestry of digital platforms, is a hyperlinked ecosystem where users generate content, share it, engage with others, and communicate fluidly across territorial boundaries or time zones. From Facebook to Twitter, Instagram to LinkedIn, YouTube to Snapchat, and more, these platforms encompass a myriad realm of human interests, emotions, and interactions. Social media is, in essence, a global township that broadcasts human existence in all its hues and colors.

## 2.2. Why Should Scientists Care?

Unraveling a double helix or deciphering the fabric of spacetime might seem more exciting than exploring the world of social media, but here's why you, as scientists, should care. Social media breaks down the fancy, intimidating glass doors of scientific research labs and brings science to the fingertips of the curious public. It allows you, as a scientist, to disseminate your research outcomes on a global scale, engage with your counterparts, participate in scientific discourses, and inspire future generations. Consequently, it amplifies scientific literacy, fuels public engagement, and fosters a collaborative scientific community, thus nurturing the dual role of a scientist: a researcher and a communicator.

## 2.3. Dissecting the Anatomy of Social media Platforms

Diving deeper into the heart of our exploration, we encounter a pulsating network of platforms, each with its use and function.

- Facebook, the most widely used platform with over 2.8 billion users, is ideal for sharing long-form content, research papers, event updates, and photos of your lab or fieldwork. Its unique features, like Groups and Pages, allow you to create closed scientific communities or public pages visible to anyone.

- Twitter, where brevity rules, enables you to share short, crisp updates about your research, join scientific conversations, follow trending hashtags, and engage with a diverse academic community.

- Instagram, a visual treat, lets you share captivating images or short videos from your experiments, lab life, field trip, or scientific conferences, thus enhancing the visual appeal of science.

- LinkedIn, a professional networking site, connects you with like-minded professionals, disseminates your research endeavors, and opens avenues for career development.

- YouTube, the prime video-sharing platform, provides a creative space to post educational videos, experimental demonstrations, or captivating documentaries about your research.

# 2.4. Leveraging Social Media: Building Bridges of Engagement

Understanding social media is one step, but how to leverage it effectively forms the crux of your exploration. Here are some strategies:

1. Be Authentic: Authenticity builds trust, humanizes science, and helps establish a loyal follower base. Share not just your successes but also the challenges, the 'Eureka' moments, and the occasional monotony of lab life.

2. Be Interactive: Engage with your audience, respond to their queries, appreciate their feedback, participate in discussions, and foster a sense of community.

3. Be Consistent: Consistency in posting content keeps your followers hooked, enhances visibility, and elevates your credibility.

4. Be Aware: Stay informed about trending hashtags, popular scientific discourses, and recent developments. Use them strategically to augment your visibility.

5. Be Respectful: Respect differing viewpoints, maintain a professional demeanor, and ensure your interactions are constructive and respectful.

In the end, remember, we are navigating a universe driven by algorithms. Understanding them, and learning to tweak them to your advantage, will define your social media journey effectively.

With these insights, the cloud of ambiguity that once shrouded social media dissipates, revealing it not as an alien planet, but a friendly neighborhood. As we advance deeper into this exploration, each layer unravels, encouraging you to wear the dual hat of a scientist and a social media maven with more confidence. Fear not the world of "Likes", "Shares", and "Tweets" dear scientists, for it is in this world, our science will find a voice that resonates beyond the sterile confines of our labs.

# Chapter 3. The Importance of Public Engagement in Science

Public engagement in science is an essential factor in bridging the gap between the scientific community and the larger public. It serves as a platform where scientists can break down complex scientific concepts into more manageable, understandable chunks for the average individual. This chapter will delve into the reasons why public engagement is crucial for scientists and their field.

## 3.1. The Power of Connective Communication

Public engagement fosters a kind of connective communication, where scientists, being the producers of scientific knowledge, engage in a conversation with the public - consumers of this knowledge. It's an interaction where both parties learn, build respect, and collaborate for better understanding and problem-solving. Through this process, scientists can appreciate societal perspectives about science, and the public can gain insights regarding how science affects and permeates their daily lives.

Engagement helps to demystify science, transforming it from an out-of-reach, enigmatic field into something tangible and relevant. When the public can relate to science, there is a higher likelihood they will support scientific endeavors, policies, and even consider career paths in the field.

## 3.2. The Role in Informing Decisions and Behaviors

A well-informed public can make sound decisions about aspects of their lives that are influenced by science and technology like health care, environmental conservation, and technological choices. Public awareness about pertinent topics like climate change, infectious diseases, or nanotechnology, empower people to make evidence-based choices and encourage a society that values and applies scientific evidence.

Moreover, it might lead to behavioral changes consistent with scientific recommendations. For instance, understanding the impact of carbon footprint might influence someone to opt for public transport over personal vehicles. These individual changes, when scaled up, can lead to significant societal improvements.

## 3.3. Building Trust and Credibility

Engaging with the public also goes a long way in establishing trust. Traditionally, there has been a gap between the scientific community and the general public attributed to several factors including complicated jargon, lack of access to scientific content, and misconceptions about scientists as individuals.

When scientists engage with the public, they become more human, accessible, and relatable. Being transparent and open about the process of science, its successes, and even its failures, can build trustworthiness. People are often supportive of those they trust, leading to public backing of scientific initiatives that might otherwise face uncertainty or opposition.

## 3.4. Encouraging Citizen Science

If there's anything more exciting than learning about science, it's contributing to it. Citizen science initiatives leverage public engagement in science, giving ordinary people a chance to participate actively in scientific research, data collection, or problem-solving. These initiatives are a validating, inclusive method of broadening scientific investigation and expanding the scientist workforce to include everyday people motivated by curiosity.

# 3.5. Conclusion

All in all, public engagement lies at the heart of science communication. It's not just a one-way dissemination of knowledge from scientists to the public. Instead, it's a dynamic, interactive dialogue that benefits both parties and society as a whole. As scientists, taking that small step out of the lab and into the realm of social media can lead to more than just likes and follows; it can foster a thriving, science-literate society, eager to learn, create, and solve.

Public engagement is not just beneficial; it's necessary. It's the kind of synergy we need, where discoveries happen in the lab and resonate with the people they ultimately impact. Engagement is science done right. It's science unconfined by lab walls, flowing into conversations, homes, schools, and policies. In the end, isn't that what we aim for?

# Chapter 4. Understanding Your Audience: A Key Ingredient for Engagement

In the invigorating realm of public engagement in the sciences, one principle stands supreme above all: the profound necessity to understand your audience. Recognizing the diverse character and dynamic tastes of your audience not only optimizes message receptivity but it also fuels the formulation of mesmerizing science narratives.

## 4.1. The Essence of Audience Analysis

Audience analysis is the act of understanding and adapting to listeners during an oral presentation or in writing, making it pivotal to your endeavours on social media. On a fundamental level, understanding audience composition can help tailor content to the audience's knowledge base, feed relatable examples that invigorate interest, and provide valuable context that bridges knowledge gaps. Audience analysis isn't a linear, one-time activity but an ongoing process that adjusts with the evolution of your audience's characteristics.

## 4.2. Profiling Your Audience: A Science in Itself

A meticulous way to understand your audience is by creating detailed audience profiles. These are deeply rooted in demographic data such as location, language, age, gender, and education, but they also entail psychographic factors such as interests, attitudes, and lifestyle preferences. An audience composed mostly of fellow scientists may appreciate posts filled with technical jargon, while an audience composed of public enthusiasts would prefer simplified explanations.

## 4.3. Leveraging Social Media Analytics

With the advent of technology, social media platforms have begun to collate vast troves of data, providing intricate insights into page followers. These analytics offer an unprecedented understanding of your audience, allowing adjustments to your strategies based on real and current data.

## 4.4. The Significance of Audience Segmentation

To navigate through the complexities of a diverse and changing audience, one effective strategy is audience segmentation. This involves dividing your overall audience into smaller groups based on certain characteristics such as demographics or interests. Audience segmentation allows for more personalized and relevant content, increasing overall engagement.

## 4.5. Tailoring Content to Match Audience Preferences

Once you understand your audience, it's necessary to tailor content accordingly to maximize appeal. For instance, younger audiences may prefer visually stimulating content that can be grasped quickly, while older audiences might favor more detailed and thought-out pieces. Similarly, recognizing time zones or active times can be decisive in having your content viewed by as many followers as possible.

## 4.6. Staying Vigilant for Audience Feedback

In the ever-fluctuating social media terrain, stasis is a curse. Constant vigilance of audience responses, content performance, and follower growth helps optimize your strategies. Upset or dissatisfied followers are not setbacks; rather, they provide constructive criticisms that can help improve your approach.

To conclude, understanding your audience is not only a key ingredient for engagement but also a critical driving force that shapes your presence in the social media landscape. It serves as the backbone for crafting content, planning dissemination strategy, and ultimately communicating the excitement of scientific exploration to the public. Embrace the dynamics of audience comprehension and unlock the extraordinary potential of public engagement in the world of science.

# Chapter 5. Mastering the Art of Crafting Your Science Story

Bracing yourself for a journey into the landscape of narrative creation, it is imperative to understand that the story of your science is the crux of public engagement on social media. Crafting an engaging narrative can radically transform dense scientific data into an enthralling tale for your audience. Mastering this art, however, is not a task achieved overnight. It requires intuitive understanding and thoughtful execution.

## 5.1. The Fabric of Storytelling and Science

First and foremost, understand that the core of successful science communication lies in the amalgamation of rigorous scientific facts and the warmth of storytelling. The juxtaposition of the two facets creates an immersive tale that transcends the boundaries of the laboratory and touches the hearts and minds of the people. The story of your work should be created with an understanding that you are not merely sharing facts; rather, you are initiating a conversation, fostering a relationship between your work and the world.

At its core, this isn't radically different from your scientific method. Just as you spend time meticulously experimenting, collecting, and analyzing data, so must you put in the effort to weave the fabric of your scientific conclusions into a comprehensible narrative. In essence, just like your research, your science story begins with a unique question or problem that you are invested to solve, progresses through experimentation (in this case, audience engagement), and concludes with an analysis, or an impactful message that warrants a call to action.

## 5.2. Utilizing the Building Blocks of a Narrative

The building blocks of any great narrative are universal: characters, setting, plot, conflict, and resolution. In the case of a scientific story, the chief character is often the scientist or the discovery itself. The landscape of your research forms the setting, while the scientific process, replete with its trials and triumphs, forms a compelling plot. The conflict arises from challenges overcome during the course of research, and the resolution is the discovery or result from your endeavor.

While the added scientific complexity might seem to complicate the storytelling process, it can rather add layers to the narrative which make it more appealing to diverse sections of your audience. For instance, the story of your discovery can be relayed in a way that highlights its potential societal impact, sparking greater curiosity and engagement by connecting the research to their everyday lives.

## 5.3. The Significance of Simplicity

Despite the complexities of your research, your story must possess an element of simplicity. The art of translating intricate scientific concepts into everyday language is a crucial aspect of crafting your science story. Always remember that your predominant aim is to shed light on your discovery, not to baffle your audience with jargon or incomprehensible data. Use metaphors and analogies; they help in making abstract scientific concepts more palpable and less intimidating.

## 5.4. Engaging Visual Content: The Catalyst

Pairing your text with visual content is a powerful strategy. A well-crafted infographic, a compelling photograph, or a short video clip magnify your storytelling prowess by leaps and bounds. Visual content enhances comprehension and boosts retention, making it an invaluable tool while breaking down complex scientific concepts.

## 5.5. The Final Equation: Feedback and Iteration

Finally, embrace feedback and continuously iterate your stories. Assess your audience's reaction and adapt your communication strategy accordingly. Remember, the process of mastering the art of crafting your science story is a journey of continuous learning and growth; it is an experiment that demands periodic analysis, revisions, and improvements.

In this journey, it may seem daunting at times, but remember, you are creating bridges between your lab and the world. You are infusing the charm of storytelling into the realm of science, rendering it accessible, relatable, and enjoyable to all. It is, indeed, a fine art that brims with satisfaction and joy upon mastery. Be patient and persistent, and with time, your lab tales can become globally loved narratives.

# Chapter 6. Tactics for Simplifying Scientific Jargon on Social Media

In the lively ecosphere of knowledge dissemination, scientists are pitted against the challenge of decoding their complex terminology into a facile, consumer-friendly language. The chapter you are reading is bedecked with strategies to solve this quandary, to intricately weave scientific jargon into the fabric of layman's discourse, using the power and reach of social media.

## 6.1. Breaking Down Complex Terms

First and foremost, the crux of an effective science communication strategy is the efficacious breakdown of complex scientific jargon. As a scientist, your dialect is laden with complicated terms and technical argot, the understanding of which remains confined within your professional circle. However, the ultimate objective of leveraging social media is to break this ring and reach the wider public who may not be adept in scientific terminology. One strategy that is widely applicable is to avoid or simplify the use of terminology that may appear arcane or esoteric to the general public. For instance, use 'water' instead of 'dihydrogen monoxide'. In situations where complicated terms are inevitable, ensure that you take time to define them accurately in your social media posts.

## 6.2. Analogies and Metaphors

A second tactic that can be adopted is the use of analogies and metaphors. This technique aids in elucidating complex concepts by paralleling them with everyday experiences that your audience can relate to. In doing so, it taps into pre-existing knowledge and understanding, making complex scientific concepts more comprehensible. An example could be explaining DNA as a 'blueprint' or 'recipe' for an organism.

## 6.3. Visual Aids and Infographics

The phrase 'a picture is worth a thousand words' is particularly germane when it comes to explaining scientific ideas. Combining text-based explanations with corresponding visual aids can vastly enhance understanding. Infographics are an exceptional resource in this regard. They can illustrate concepts, processes, or statistical data in a creative, visually striking format which can aid in both engagement and comprehension.

## 6.4. The Power of Storytelling

Storytelling has been used as a tool for teaching and learning throughout history. Narratives enable listeners to identify with characters and their struggles, rendering the entire process more accessible and engaging. Incorporating this approach, scientists can weave their findings, theories, or data into compelling narratives. For instance, tracing the journey of a scientific discovery, the problems encountered, and how the knowledge has evolved over time can turn an otherwise dry scientific update into a gripping narrative.

## 6.5. Leverage Influencers and Collaborators

Recognizing the influence of more popular figures in the community and involving them in your communication can be an effective approach. Owing to their established reputation, scientists and science communicators with a larger following can expand the reach of your message, and their endorsement can lend credibility to your work. Collaborating with popular science communication platforms can also help demystify scientific jargon and highlight the essence of your work.

# 6.6. Use of Humor and Emotive Language

Finally, incorporating humor and emotive language into your communication can make it more engaging. Scientific descriptions tend to be dry and impersonal; however, humanizing these descriptions, eliciting emotions and utilizing playful undertones can greatly enhance audience engagement.

In conclusion, simplifying scientific jargon for social media consumption requires a conscious effort to break away from entrenched academic habits. Choosing simple, everyday language, using analogies and metaphors, leveraging visual aids, storytelling, influencers, and emotive language are ways to make complicated scientific ideas accessible and engaging to the layperson. This is by no means an easy task; however, it is an essential element of effectively communicating science to the public.

# Chapter 7. Effective Social Media Platforms for Scientists

In the vast universe of social media, numerous platforms provide unique opportunities for scientists to share their work, engage in dialogue with the public, enhance visibility and generate impact. However, each platform possesses its own strengths, weaknesses, audience, and cultures. In turn, this requires you, as a scientist, to fashion your content befitting each platform to leverage its full potential. This exploration will be your guide through the thickets of these platforms.

## 7.1. Diving into the World of Twitter

Twitter, a microblogging platform, has soared over the digital world as a potent tool for disseminating scientific knowledge. Here, every tweet is capped at 280 characters, demanding brevity; yet, with judicious crafting, your science can unravel bite-sized information, threads for longer narratives, interactive quizzes, and more, offering multiple pathways to capture the fleeting attention of the scrollers.

Twitter is filled with an active scientific community, scholars, journalists, policymakers, and an increasingly science-curious public, making it a desirable platform. Utilizing hashtags effectively, such as #scicomm, #phdchat, or specific tags during scientific conferences can help cast your ideas in the right spaces. Furthermore, Twitter promotes real-time interaction, enabling users to engage directly with scientists, fostering dialogue and potentially demystifying the complex world of scientific research.

# 7.2. Deciphering the World of Facebook

Facebook, one of the oldest social media platforms, is characterized by a high user volume, creating a vast sea of potential target audience. Its power is in the capacity to form dedicated groups, permitting increased interaction between like minds. This platform is effective for sharing longer narratives, image galleries, links to blogs, and videos.

Hosting live sessions, webinars, or Q&As are immensely popular on Facebook. These are excellent opportunities to present your work in an interactive format, answering direct questions from viewers. Facebook is suitable for longer engagements compared to Twitter, facilitating detailed conversations about your research.

# 7.3. Navigating through Instagram

Instagram thrives on visually compelling content. Particularly for areas of science where visuals carry an immense narrative punch, such as microscopy, astronomy, or field biology, this platform can be incredibly effective. Infographics explainer videos, and stunning images can communicate your science in captivating ways.

Instagram Stories and Reels, with their temporal nature, allow for more informal or behind-the-scenes content. These features can provide a glimpse into the life of a scientist, humanizing the process of science, and fostering a closer connection with the audience.

# 7.4. LinkedIn – The Professional's Playground

As a professional networking site, LinkedIn holds a slightly formal demeanor, making it an ideal platform for sharing job updates, professional achievements, research papers, and to network with other researchers, businesses, or industry professionals. Its audience is primed for receiving more industry-oriented content, and engagement tends to be in the context of job opportunities, collaboration, and business partnerships.

## 7.5. Venturing into YouTube

YouTube, as a video-sharing platform, is valuable for illustrating scientific phenomena that demand more than jargon-filled explanations. With the aid of animations, field footage, interviews, or explainer videos, YouTube offers the capability to convey intricate processes in understandable and engaging ways.

It caters to the preference of visuals over text, satiating the public's appetite for consumable science. Hosting webinars, lectures, and virtual tours of your lab can be accomplished effortlessly on this platform. Despite the higher production value required, the payoff can be considerable.

## 7.6. Riding the Wave of Podcasts

The growth of audio-content platforms such as Spotify or Apple Podcasts has opened novel avenues for scientific communication. Crafting science podcasts can allow for deep dives into topics that are ordinarily complex to unravel in shorter formats. They allow for interviews with experts, discussions on nuanced subjects, and storytelling, all in an easily digestible auditory format.

Each social media platform caters to different user behavior and content format preferences. For scientists looking to enhance their public outreach or engagement, these platforms offer the ability to connect with a variety of demographic segments, and share their research in adaptable and creative ways.

# Chapter 8. Building Your Science Brand on Social Media

Building a robust and recognizable science brand on social media entails a strategic orchestration of various elements to create a unique identity in the digital sphere. It is the process of developing a distinguishable persona that echoes your scientific expertise, philosophy, and skills through online platforms. In this chapter, we will elucidate the importance of developing a strong science brand, explain the stages of brand-building, and dive deep into strategies that can make your scientific brand stand out in the bustling social media landscape.

## 8.1. Understanding the Concept of a Science Brand

A science brand is essentially the scientific persona you project to the digital world. It represents your scientific perspectives, accomplishments, research interests, and values that are encapsulated within your digital presence. It is what distinguishes you from a throng of fellow researchers and scientists across social media platforms. A well-crafted science brand makes you recognizable within a boundaryless digital realm, increases the potential that your work will be discovered, and encourages audience engagement on a wider scale.

# 8.2. Steps to Cultivate Your Science Brand

The process of building your science brand is not an overnight achievement but an evolution that takes growth and learning. However, by adhering systematically to these simple steps, you can expedite the process:

1. Ascertain your brand's purpose: Recognize what you want to achieve with your scientific work; it may be encouraging public engagement in scientific research, making your research more accessible, or educating the public about specific scientific concepts.

2. Identify your unique selling proposition (USP): Discover what distinguishes you from your fellow scientists. It may be your specific area of expertise, your unique perspective on scientific matters, or your distinct communication style.

3. Define your target audience: Consider who you wish to reach with your scientific brand—are they students, fellow researchers, science enthusiasts, or the general public?

4. Create a consistent brand voice and image: Consistency in your tone, language, and visuals aids in creating a recognizable brand. From the colors and fonts used in your graphics to the tone and style of your writing, consistency is key.

5. Interact and engage with your audience: Social media is not a one-way communication channel. Frequent interaction with your audience through comments, likes, and shares helps strengthen your brand's presence and builds a loyal and engaged community.

# 8.3. Employing the Right Strategies to Build Your Science Brand

Creating a powerful science brand on social media involves multiple strategies synced together in harmony. These strategies can be broadly classified into the following categories:

1. Strong Visual Branding: Ensure a cohesive, aesthetically pleasing visual brand across all social media platforms. Use consistent colors, fonts, aesthetics, and postings. Every visual component should feel searchable, identifiable, and unique to your brand, signalling professionalism and thoughtfulness.

2. Compelling Content Creation: Create enticing content that brings your scientific brand's unique facets to the fore. Diversify your content in styles and formats; go for blogs, reels, infographics, whitepapers, podcasts, etc., pertinent to the platform you choose. Remember, content is king when it comes to brand-building.

3. Consistency and Frequency: Maintaining regular posting schedules and sticking to a consistent tone and style of communication helps to build trust and fosters familiarity.

4. Fostering Engagement: Authentic, meaningful conversations with your audience can help your science brand thrive. Empathize with their concerns and provide satisfactory answers to their queries to build a rapport and humanize your brand.

# 8.4. Adapting Your Social Media Presence to Your Science Brand

It's essential that your science brand image is reflected in your social media strategies. Optimize your profile for your brand persona, customize your profile and cover photos to reflect the visual aspects of your brand, and be sure to have your biography express your brand's unique aspects. Also, don't forget to include key information such as the field of your expertise, your key accomplishments and publications, and a link to your professional webpage if applicable.

## 8.5. Navigating Challenges in Building Your Science Brand

Though building a science brand on social media offers many benefits, certain challenges might arise during the process. Concerns such as time commitments, negative feedback or trolling, and evolving digital trends can pose potential hurdles. However, with strategic planning, these challenges can be navigated smoothly. Managing time by creating content in blocks and scheduling posts, fostering a culture of empathy and respectful communication, and staying updated with digital trends can all mitigate these concerns.

As you can see, building your science brand on social media takes time, strategic thinking, a dash of creativity, and heaps of consistency. However, the rewards make the journey worthwhile. It enhances your visibility, fosters meaningful connections with a wider audience, and carves a unique space for you in the bustling digital world. Engaging with the public through a strong science brand can contribute meaningfully to science communication, research ends, and can foster enhanced understanding and appreciation for science in the wider society. Endeavor to develop and cultivate your science brand, and watch it flourish in the dynamic world of social media.

# Chapter 9. Social Media Metrics: Measuring Engagement Success

The multifaceted realm of social media metrics can be as complex and diverse as a scientist's research project. Nevertheless, understanding this realm is pivotal in mastering the art of using social media platforms to engage with the broader public concerning scientific research. From amassing followers, charting engagement rates, to tracking the reach of your posts, a meticulous understanding of these metrics is an invaluable tool for the savvy scientist in the age of digital interaction.

## 9.1. Unraveling the Web: Understanding Social Media Metrics

Social media metrics are varied and extensive, directly reflecting the multifaceted nature of digital platforms. While specific metrics might differ across platforms, multiple universal indicators include likes, shares, comments, follows/followers, and post reach. These indicators help users gauge the level of interaction and engagement their content is generating.

**Likes** are the simplest form of engagement, encapsulating a user's interest or appreciation for a post.

**Shares** are another vital metric, indicating a compelling level of engagement that prompted the user to disseminate your post beyond their network, amplifying your message reach.

**Comments** often present a more profound level of engagement, suggesting that your content has incited a reaction or thought that the user felt compelled to express.

**Follows/Followers**, while a more passive form of engagement, delineate a consistent interest in your content that could potentially translate into longer-term engagement.

**Post Reach** is an all-encompassing metric that gives you an idea of the extent of your content's visibility, with a higher reach correlating with visibility to a broader audience base.

## 9.2. The Metrics Cocktail: Selecting the Relevant Metrics

As a scientist adventuring in the labyrinth of social media, it's necessary to identify and focus on the metrics that best align with your goals. For instant, if the objective is to increase awareness about a specific subject, the relevant metrics to emphasize would be Reach and Shares. Conversely, if the focus is on fostering discussions and debates, one might prioritize the number of Comments.

While most social media platforms provide basic insights into these metrics, advanced tools can offer a more nuanced understanding of these metrics and their interplay. Services like Hootsuite, Buffer, and Sprout Social can help drill down into specifics such as the demographics of users who engage with your posts, peak times for user interaction, or comparing performance across different posts.

## 9.3. Interpreting Metrics: The Art and Science

In the realm of social media, raw numbers are the science, while their interpretation is the art. The crux of making these metrics meaningful lies in adeptly interpreting them to evaluate and refine your strategy. A dip in engagement might signal the need to revisit and revamp your content, while a spike could indicate an area you can emphasize more, building on its success.

It's imperative not to get too caught up in the numbers game. While higher metrics are often desirable, quality should take precedence over quantity. A smaller, more engaged audience is leagues better than a massive, disinterested one. The most compelling metrics should always be those that indicate genuine, resonating engagement with your content.

# 9.4. Overcoming Missteps: Tweaking Your Strategy

One of the unique aspects of social media engagement lies in its dynamic and iterative nature. If certain metrics aren't aligning with your expectations or objectives, it's not a setback but an opportunity to retune your approach.

For instance, low reach could be combated with hashtag optimization or collaborations with accounts boasting larger followings. Low engagement could hint at the need for more interactive or visually appealing content, like infographics or videos. This constant feedback loop is one of social media's most powerful features.

# 9.5. Social Media Metrics: The Future Prospect

The expansive arena of social media metrics continuously evolves as platforms innovate and as audience behaviors shift. For instance, new metrics such as Saves on Instagram or Impressions on Twitter add further layers to this complex tapestry. As technologies like machine learning and AI come into play, we might soon have predictive metrics offering foresight into engagement trends.

Diving into social media as a scientist can seem arduous at first, yet, with a persistent approach backed by understanding and analyzing your social media metrics, it's an endeavor poised to enrich your engagement with the public. After all, the beauty of science lies not just within the confines of a lab, but also in its ability to fascinate, inspire and foster discussions. Social Media Metrics, therefore, isn't an end in itself; it's a means to a far more remarkable end - bridging science and society.

# Chapter 10. Overcoming Challenges: Dealing with Misinformation and Criticism

In a discourse most fortunate and timely, we embark upon navigating the treacherous terrains of misinformation and criticism, obstinately pervasive across the sprawling plains of social media. As agents of science and purveyors of factual knowledge, it is within your intrepid capability to rise above these challenges, equipped with your toolkits brimming with sage strategies and insightful advice.

## 10.1. Dealing with Misinformation

The lurking behemoth of misinformation unfailingly finds solace in the labyrinthine alleys of social media platforms. Often manufactured inadvertently due to a misunderstanding of the complex scientific phenomenon, and at times commissioned willfully to breed discord, misinformation is an adversary to factual dialogue and progress.

In dealing with misinformation, there are four canny methods you might employ, each designed to combat the distortions with a particular approach:

1. Address misinformation directly: Advancing frontally yet respectfully, directly clarify the misinformation without resorting to aggression or condescension.

2. Simplify your message: Ensuring that your scientific information is distilled to the level that can be comprehended by a common reader significantly reduces the space for misinterpretation and consequent misinformation.

3. Engage with popular social media influencers: Undeniably, social media influencers command a large following. Allying with them lets you address misinformation on a grand scale, enabling checkmate on the damaging spread of inaccuracies.

4. Create visual content: The human brain processes visuals faster and more effectively than text. Armed with the science of cognition and perception, try transforming your complex scientific findings into graphs, diagrams, or animations.

# 10.2. Responding to Criticism

The companion on your social media journey, flanking misinformation, is criticism. Often emerging as unsolicited comments from people with differing perspectives or understanding, it is key to approach this with equanimity and tact. After all, criticism, when navigated deftly, may serve as a crucible for refinement and growth.

The line that divides constructive criticism from baseless fault-finding can often blur, but adhering to the following tenets can facilitate a productive outcome:

1. Stay composed: In the face of criticism, remember not to let emotions overshadow rationality. Engage with the criticism objectively.

2. Appreciate constructive criticism: Encourage dialogue with those presenting reasoned critiques. Engage, respond, and reciprocate with appreciative cues to encourage positive interactions.

3. Negate personal attacks politely: Not every criticism is constructive. Ensure you differentiate and negate personal attacks or baseless criticism in a firm yet polite manner.

4. Use peer-reviewed research to support your claim: There may be instances when criticism arises due to misunderstanding or lack of understanding. In such scenarios, references to peer-reviewed research can significantly affirm your stance.

## 10.3. Building Resilience and Encouraging Dialogue

Brimming with the potential to be both a constructive crucible and destructive wildfire, the social media landscape for scientific discourses is fraught with challenges. Building resilience to criticism and misinformation, while continuously engaging in dialogue with your audience, can lay the foundation for a successful social engagement strategy.

A preemptive to these challenges begins with anticipating potential criticism and misinformation, and crafting messages that pre-address these concerns. Encourage open dialogue, invite perspectives, and instill a sense of community. The more individuals that partake in the discussion, the more holistic the understanding of the subject becomes.

Promote fact-checking cultures among your followers and use your platform not just to share your findings, but also to teach how to discern fact from fiction. Proactively addressing potential conflicts, coupled with a zealous commitment to spreading knowledge, can help build an informed and resilient audience.

As the final curtain falls on this chapter, remember that the ride across the social media terrain, while indeed bumpy at times, is an exhilarating journey of learning, sharing, and engagement that will only enrich your scientific pursuits. We recognize the challenges, but armed with patience, respect, resilience, and a commitment to fostering an informed dialogue, you are undoubtedly on the path to overcoming these obstacles, ever poised to engage effectively beyond the lab.

# Chapter 11. Future Prospects of Social Media in Science Communication

As we stand on the sweeping horizon of the digital age, it's increasingly important to recognize the expansive role that social media can and does play in the dissemination of scientific knowledge. Its influence is ubiquitous, pervasive, and transformative, shifting the paradigms of communication by creating dynamic platforms where scientists can share their work with the public in a more intimate, interactive, and engaging manner.

## 11.1. The Unrivaled Power of Connectivity

Increasing connectivity is one of the most significant advantages offered by social media platforms. With nearly half of the global population using social media, scientists have the potential to reach an unprecedented audience. More importantly, social media has the capacity to connect scientists not only to those within their immediate circle but also to a broader network of colleagues, influencers, thought leaders, educators, policy-makers, and the general public. This ability to bridge the gap between the scientific community and the public sphere is fundamental for developing a culture that understands, accepts, and engages with science.

## 11.2. Peer-Peer Influence & Dialogue Enhancement

Social media platforms provide an avenue for scientists to address misconceived notions about scientific concepts, by directly conveying accurate information. This direct line of communication serves as a powerful tool in debunking myths and false information, thus promoting scientific facts over harmful misinformation or misunderstanding.

## 11.3. Real-Time Engagement

With the ability to share real-time updates and inputs, social media offers the unique advantage of speed and timeliness in terms of disseminating scientific information. This opens avenues for live dialogues, webinars, Q&A sessions, and virtual conferences that can be accessed globally in real time or at the convenience of the users.

## 11.4. The Democratization of Science

Social media is hence transforming what traditionally has been a one-way flow of information into a two-way dialogue, enabling the democratization of science. It encourages different voices, ensures transparency, and empowers people to actively participate in scientific discussions and decision making processes.

## 11.5. Digitally Scientific: The Road Ahead

Analyzing the possibilities of social media's role in the future of scientific communication is akin to listening to a symphony of interconnected trends and patterns. The digitalization of scientific communication is also intrinsically linked to the progress of technology advancements.

## 11.6. The Advent of The Social Scientist

The future points towards the rise of the 'social scientist' - theorists and professionals who embrace the fusion of science with the digital sphere. These individuals would exhibit a balance of scientific expertise and communication skills, tailoring information for various social media platforms.

## 11.7. Accelerating AI in Scientific Communications

The advancement in Artificial Intelligence (AI) and machine learning technologies are set to transform social media, revamping static platforms into interactive personalized conduits of information. With AI-driven hashtags, trends, and content suggestions, social media platforms could potentially become personalized learning platforms for scientists and the public alike.

## 11.8. Harnessing Augmented & Virtual Reality

In the future, the utilization of Augmented Reality (AR) and Virtual Reality (VR) technology on social media platforms could provide immersive experiences for audiences. Scientists could harness these technologies to visually represent complex scientific concepts and phenomena, thereby enhancing the understanding and engagement.

## 11.9. Bots & Echo Chambers

While we look towards the future with optimism, it is important to be cognizant of the potential challenges. The ever-looming specter of bots spreading misinformation and the creation of echo chambers where false information can flourish are critical issues to be addressed both now and in the future.

# 11.10. Overcoming Challenges: Future Implications

While acknowledging potential difficulties, we must employ strategic and tactical approaches in mitigating the challenges we face, from developing comprehensive social media policies, promoting scientific media literacy, to improving algorithms for better information dissemination.

Overall, the potential for social media's role in the scientific communication landscape is immense and ever-expanding. As we venture further into the realms of the virtual world, it's incumbent upon us to harness its potential responsibly and creatively. Ensuring the accuracy and reach of scientific communication, promoting dialogue, and fostering a culture of learning and engagement are key factors. With exciting prospects and challenges head, let's stride forward, collaboratively working towards shaping future trajectories, catalyzing advancements, and harmonizing science with social media, as we usher in a democratized era of scientific communication.